TO FLY TO SERVE

TO FLY TO SERVE

Practical help for giving a Bible talk

Adrian Reynolds

10 Publishing
a division of 10 of those.com

First published in Great Britain in 2016

British Library Cataloguing in Publication Data
A record for this book is available from the British Library

ISBN: 978-1-910587-60-7

Designed by Diane Warnes

Printed in the UK by CPI

10Publishing, a division of 10ofthose.com
Unit C, Tomlinson Road, Leyland, PR25 2DY, England
Email: info@10ofthose.com
Website: www.10ofthose.com

CONTENTS

SERIES INTRODUCTION

The Hub Conference was launched in 2013 by the Fellowship of Independent Evangelical Churches (FIEC) as an annual conference to help men and women find clear routes into Independent church ministry. For those 'just looking' as well as those 'just started', The Hub aims to be one means of support and advice on a possible journey through training and into gospel ministry.

Led by experienced gospel workers from the FIEC, and supported by leaders from colleges and courses, The Hub provides Bible ministry and a wide range of seminars on ministry-related issues.

It is out of this annual conference that this series of books was born. It occurred to the organising committee that these seminar topics could provide a helpful resource for anyone involved in gospel ministry, whether or not they attended The Hub or entered paid Christian ministry. In addition, the hope is that these books might also help pastors and leaders in discipling members of congregations for leadership and ministry.

Someone once described theological books as a *'college of teachers committed to helping you do your best to handle the Word of truth'*. We hope this series will play a small but significant part in that library of wisdom, at whatever stage you find yourself.

We are thrilled that Adrian Reynolds has written the next book in the series, on giving a Bible talk. As you will soon discover, Adrian's focus is on anyone involved in teaching the gospel in whatever context that might be – from Sunday sermon to Sunday school class; from small group to youth fellowship. In fact, wherever and whenever a Bible talk is given, this book will be of immense help.

Trevor Archer and Dan Green
Series editors

fiec
the FELLOWSHIP of INDEPENDENT EVANGELICAL CHURCHES

INTRODUCTION

TO FLY TO SERVE

In 2011 British Airways, the UK's national airline, adopted a new marketing strategy. Gone was the phrase 'The world's favourite airline' (principally because they weren't any more) and instead was the rather more mysterious 'To fly. To serve.' BA wanted to try to reintroduce something of the magic of flying, harking back to a bygone age when aeroplanes were cruise liners in the sky. The slogan (emblazoned on the BA cap) was accompanied by a slick marketing campaign with soft-focus shots and happy children holding the hands of handsome pilots.

The pilots and crew, we were assured, were there to serve us. That's what they lived for; that's what they flew for. Now call me a cynic but I think that BA is probably just as interested in commercial practicalities – like profits. Still, I suppose it's a good sentiment.

Right now, you may be a bit puzzled. This isn't quite the start you expected. And in the remote and unlikely event that you expected a book about flying a plane, I'm doubly sorry. Right now as I write this, believe it or not, I'm actually *on* a plane. I would love to be in the cockpit, surveying the scene. Maybe we think flying sounds glamorous. However, what we need to understand is that this short book is about something *more* glamorous: something with *more* potential for excitement and something that will take people from A to B where B is the most delightful, exciting, incredible and – above all – eternal destination.

'To fly. To serve' is a great sentiment for BA, despite my cynicism. And it's also a great attitude for every man or woman who is asked to come and speak from the Bible. The focus on service for BA is to get you from A to B comfortably, safely and happily. The Bible speaker has many of the same goals. He (or she, in the appropriate setting) wants to get the hearers to a certain destination, of which more in a moment. His aim in speaking is not to draw attention to himself. Nor is it to give hearers a kind of fairground ride. There are, if you like, a lot of similarities and I'm going to use these to develop some helpful guidelines for giving a Bible talk.

This book, then, is essentially one long parable. Perhaps, at times, you will feel that I'm pushing it too far. That may be so. But as long as you take on board the lessons and let them sink in, I'm not really too bothered.

Flying a plane? Ha! That's nothing! This is a short book about something miles better: giving a Bible talk.

WHAT'S IN A WORD?

By using the phrase 'Bible talk' I've tried to be as general as possible. I want this help to cover those who are preaching, doing a short talk at a Christian Union, leading a Bible study, introducing an evangelistic Bible study and even taking a Sunday school lesson. I happen to believe that, in every case, the language of 'talk' is not really quite the thing. Preaching, in particular, should never be relegated to using this kind of language. Even the humble study with just a few participants is not adequately described using this wording. Nevertheless, I wanted a description that would capture everything, and for the moment 'Bible talk' is it. Please work with it!

MISSING PIECES

You've probably already noticed that this is a short book. It means it's going to be pretty useless to prop open a door, or to impress your friends with, 'Look what I'm reading!' I recommend *War and Peace* – in hardback, of course – for both of those tasks. If this book is not being used as a doorstop or a crowd-puller, then it means that you're probably going to have to read it. So let me break one piece of news to you before you begin.

I'm not going to say anything – or very little, anyway – about how to actually understand a Bible text. There are several reasons for that. First, there are lots of very good books about that already. I've listed some of them at the end. There are also good courses and online materials you can access which will help you with this. Second, I don't want to distract from the main purpose of this book. There are lots of people who are simply excellent at interpreting Bible texts and passages. They have letters after their names and often a few in front too. I've benefited from them hugely. But teaching others is more than understanding the text (though never less). That's why I'm going to focus on the practicalities of actually giving a Bible talk.

Also, and most importantly, you'll not find any technical jargon. I preached my first sermon aged eighteen as a fresh-faced first-year university student. I don't think the small church where I was worshipping (as the only student) knew quite what had hit them – they got the whole of Habakkuk (that's quite a lot of prophecy) in one go. What I really needed was training or a book just like this. I'm writing it, I guess, for my younger self. So in it there's no mention of exegesis, eisegesis, homiletics and historical-grammatical methods, but just plain old English.

HOLY SPIRIT, WHERE ART THOU?

There's one other key omission from this book and I need to explain it. I will say nothing more beyond this short section about the work of the Holy Spirit in speaking God's word. That's not because I don't believe in him! No, quite the opposite. I believe any Bible speaker in any setting must be prayerfully dependent on the power of the Spirit in their preparation and delivery, beforehand and afterwards. Only when he is at work will anything happen.

But neither should a solid belief in the work of the Spirit stop us from thinking and planning our talks carefully. After all, we don't revert to such fatalism in any other area of life. We don't close our eyes whilst driving in the mistaken belief that the Spirit will guide us through. No, we are not fatalists, like Muslims.

So we work hard at understanding the text and (what I'm really interested in here) delivering a talk that is tuned so that it is easy to hear and take in.

RULES ARE MADE TO BE BROKEN

This is a book for first-timers – those just starting out on Bible talks – or those who want to get a few ideas to do something better they're already doing. That's not to say that experienced speakers won't benefit. Some old-timers get into bad habits that need certain realignment every now and again. I should know – I'm one of them.

The tips in this book are not hard and fast rules, but rather a wise starting point. So please hear me clearly: I'm not giving you the Ten Commandments of public speaking. However, what I trust you will find here are helpful ideas or – at a stretch – guidelines that will improve your Bible talk.

But don't fasten your seat belt just yet. First, let's get out the holiday brochure ...

DESTINATION

WHERE DO YOU FANCY GOING?

That flight I just told you about, the one I am on, is heading for Washington DC, Dulles Airport. I'm off to the US for a preaching conference. At least, I *hope* that's where we're heading. Frankly, if we land in a few hours' time and I find myself in Chicago, Illinois, I'm going to be pretty hacked off (no offence to the dear people of the Windy City). The pilot is there to fly the plane to the destination already fixed by the airline and its schedulers – he has no right to change his mind about where he lands. And we, the paid-up passengers, fully expect that the pilot will serve us best by taking us where he is told to go by his superiors.

Any person who speaks from the Bible may feel that they're in the captain's seat. To a certain extent that is true. Take a preacher, for example. He can determine the length of the sermon; he's responsible for the content; he decides what illustrations to add in; he works through the application; and he brings the sermon to a good conclusion.

But the one thing a preacher is not at liberty to do is to determine the destination. Let me explain. We believe the Bible to be God's word. Indeed, this is the Bible's own testimony about itself:

> **All Scripture is God-breathed and is useful for teaching, rebuking, correcting and training in righteousness, so that the servant of God may be thoroughly equipped for every good work. (2 Tim. 3:16-17)**

What, exactly, then, is going on when we speak from the Bible in any setting? We're not saying anything new. We can't be – that would put us on a level *with* God himself. We're not taking our own views and imposing them on a Bible text to give them some justification – that would put us on a level *above* God. Nor are we ignoring the Bible and just doing our own thing. I have heard sermons like that where the preacher reads out a text, closes the Bible and then says, in effect, 'And now for something completely different.'

As I've already said, this isn't going to be a book about how to understand a Bible passage or text. But we do need to say, right at the outset, that when you're giving a Bible talk, you're giving God the microphone (as one of my colleagues likes to put it). You are not setting the agenda, or being cutting edge, or starting a revolution of your own.

You're the messenger, the herald, the ambassador – who is there to represent what the King wants to say. You're the pilot. So don't sit on the runway and say to yourself, 'You know, I'd really rather go somewhere else today.' Don't do your pre-flight checks and think, 'What this crowd needs is a bit of a surprise!' Remember the motto 'To fly. To serve.' You're serving these people and the best way you can do that is to take them to the destination that your superior officer has already determined.

NO SOFT OPTION

Being such a pilot requires some hard work in getting ready. I used to think that a pilot had a pretty cushy job, sitting up there in the cockpit. He got a smart uniform and some cool shades. Then I met one or two and discovered how wrong I was. It's not just that the flight itself (boring though it sometimes is) is exhausting. It's not even because of the nervous energy that take-off and landing bring. No, it's also the unseen work that must happen beforehand. They must know precisely where they're going and the details of the airport. They need to work out the fuel load and check the weather to make sure they're going to be able to give passengers a smooth flight. It's all of this and more.

The man or woman giving a Bible talk needs to invest the same amount of hard work. In that same letter, Paul writes to young pastor Timothy:

> **Do your best to present yourself to God as one approved, a worker who does not need to be ashamed and who correctly handles the word of truth. (2 Tim. 2:15)**

Do you see the language? 'Do your best' and 'worker'. Giving a Bible talk is no walk in the park. And here's the big hit: it's actually harder for you than it is for many people who speak week in, week out. There are certain approaches and disciplines that they're used to. They are often paid to do this – they have time during the week, whilst you're out slaving from 9 to 5 (or worse), get home, see the wife and kids, attend the church prayer meeting and *then* get around to prep. So don't underestimate the preparation task.

It's a key task – because it's the hard work beforehand that will give you the right destination. And if you fly your passengers to the wrong place, well, you're not really helping them at all, are you? In fact, you may actually be doing them more damage than you can possible imagine.

Well, the destination is set – let's assume you've now got it right after all your preparation. What next? It's time to strap yourself in and get ready to go. It's time, in fact, for take-off.

TAKE-OFF

DANGEROUS MOMENTS

My friends who are pilots or who know anything about this tell me that the take-off and landing are the most dangerous moments of any flight. That's pretty obvious when you stop and think about it. It's the moment when most stresses are put on the plane and when the capabilities of the crew are tested to the limit.

Take-off and landing are also critical moments for passengers. Any flight is likely to be made up of a real mixture of customers. There will be regular travellers, probably in the more expensive seats. These are the guys who travel on business, perhaps once a week, and listen disdainfully to the safety announcements. There are other less regular travellers who love flying. They love the drama, the smell of aviation fuel that pervades every airport and the thought that they can pay hundreds of pounds to watch a movie on a tiny screen rather than a much smaller amount to go to the local cinema! I think you can tell I'm not in this category.

There are others who are indifferent to travel. It's just something to get them from A to B, and as long as they get to B they don't care a whole heap about the bit in-between. There are still others who are terrified. Perhaps this is their first time flying. Perhaps they've flown plenty but some bad experiences (or bad memories) make them more nervous each time they fly. Perhaps if you've ever flown you would recognise yourself in these categories?

It may not surprise you to hear, then, that in front of you as you give your Bible talk are all kinds of hearers. Some will be for you. Some may well be against you. Some will be willing you on. Some will be wishing you were finished. Some will be excited and love hearing anyone unpack the Bible. Others may find it the most trying chore of the week. Your job is to get them all in the air.

In other words, the take-off really counts. It is the moment when the passengers get going. It is the moment when they get an idea of just how competent the pilot is. Perhaps he comes on the intercom and they are able to be reassured by his tone of voice or calm manner? Unless the pilot gets people safely into the air, the flight will be a disaster. Likewise you need to engage your audience and get them started in the right direction.

PUT PEOPLE AT EASE

A take-off in a Bible talk is the introduction. It is the very first part of your talk and it really, really counts. For what it's worth, I think it is *so* important that it should be left until the end of your preparation. That's certainly what I try to do. I don't quite trust myself enough to think of a good opening first. The danger is I will hang everything else on it, and end up giving an Adrian-talk not a Bible-talk.

And though it should not be contrived or forced, nevertheless a good introduction does need to draw people in. It needs to settle and, if necessary, provide some reassurance. Knowing just how to do that is often a function of knowing who is in front of you.

That's not a whole heap different from being captain of a plane. A captain who knows he has a lot of nervous flyers will say something on the intercom to help. A pilot who knows his plane is full of holidaymakers heading off to the Seychelles may say something to help the holiday spirit along.

Let's say you're preaching on Ephesians 2:1–10. Your introduction will sound different in an evangelistic talk than it will if it's a Sunday morning sermon to a congregation of mature believers. The former might start with a story about how dead a frozen chicken is: nothing will bring it to life! However, a Sunday sermon might start by asking people to remember back to when they were not Christians.

Alternatively, perhaps your church has just been through some terrible tragedy? Then a sermon on Job 1 to them will have a different introduction (perhaps about how God's word speaks into this situation) from a sermon to a group of young business people who all think they're indestructible (where the suddenness and shock of Job's loss would be a more appropriate beginning). Do you get the idea?

Your talk take-off has to draw all these people in. That's a tall order, so here are a few guidelines to make a good start.

TAKE OFF IN THE RIGHT DIRECTION

The airspace around Washington is crowded. Unlike London, two of its largest airports are so close that you can see the planes from the other location climbing up from the runway and making sharp turns. I don't know about you, but sudden turns in aircraft make me nervous. I like the kind of flight where the plane takes off in the direction it will eventually go.

Now, I know that's not always possible. There are all kinds of reasons why planes have to take off the opposite way from the way they're headed and then make some sharp banks. But, all the same, I'd rather they didn't. Flying in a straight line is always better for passengers.

And it's always better for your Bible hearers if you start the way you mean to go on. What I mean is this: your introduction should serve the rest of the message. It needs to take people in the same direction. You don't want to be preaching 1 Corinthians 13 (about love) and start with an illustration on barbeques. There will be too many changes of direction involved and people will be lost before you even begin.

This is one of the hardest things to get right in a Bible talk. We know the beginning is important, but it's a difficult thing to carry off. There are books and books of introductions and illustrations which people sometimes try to shoehorn in to fit the passage, but the best kind of illustrations are those which carry your passengers in the right direction.

Let me just add that negative illustrations rarely help do that. It's always easier to find a negative story rather than a positive one. To change the metaphor a little, a carrot is – positively – only one thing: a carrot. But negatively it is thousands of things: it is not an orange, nor a lifeboat, nor a smoothie, nor a big bushy red beard. And knowing it is none of those things does not actually tell you a whole heap about it. So don't start your talk with a great story about something or other and then utter the line, 'Our passage today is *not* like that.' That's too much of a steep turn.

Nor do you want your introduction to grate with the rest of the message. It's not just the direction that's important. If you have a sober passage, for example Job 1, you will not serve anybody by starting with, 'Let me tell you the funniest story I have ever heard.' No, a good introduction for Job is going to draw people into the blackness and shock of the story.

ACCELERATE QUICKLY AND CLIMB TO ALTITUDE

Introductions should not, on the whole, take too long. Personally, on an aeroplane, I want the 'Fasten your seat belts' sign to go off as quickly as possible. There is something reassuring about knowing we are no longer in the danger zone of take-off. Then the quicker we reach our cruising altitude of, say, 30,000 feet, the quicker we will get there.

Of course the huge lumbering aircraft that fly for vast distances need a long run to get airborne. Nevertheless, the chances are most of your first Bible talks are more likely to be short haul in comparison. Although you may be given an hour-long slot, it is unlikely. Therefore, the best advice is to get in the air quickly. Good pilots know that the distance is best covered in level flight. The take-off may be memorable, but it needs to be swift.

A lot of Bible talks spend too much time on the runway. Listening to some, I wonder whether they will ever get in the air at all. To use a completely different picture – a golfing metaphor – one of my colleagues calls this waggling on the tee. He's been training preachers for decades, and yet he told me just last week that he still hears a lot of waggling going on.

Just think about this for a moment. What do introductions do? They introduce, of course. They introduce themes, direction, tone and pace. They give hearers confidence in the message that will come. They help listeners think, 'Yes, this is something I ought to pay attention to.' That means that long introductions will always rob the talk of the time it needs to do the work God wants to do in the text.

Introductions *introduce* the text, but they are *not* the text. So the preacher who keeps you revving the engines on the runway, or waggling on the tee, or whatever other picture you like to use, will never really be giving his hearers what they most need – which is to get deeply into God's word. That's what I call level flight and it comes next.

LEVEL FLIGHT

SLOW AND STEADY

I grew up in Southend-on-Sea which, until recently, hosted an annual air show. We used to line up on the cliffs by the seafront, sitting on our picnic rugs and watching the planes fly down the Thames Estuary. It was quite a sight and the raked vantage point meant that we got the best view of the acrobatics. I guess every small boy wanted to be in one of those planes as they looped the loop.

Similarly, once you get into the text you've got to preach or teach, you might feel sorely tempted to give people your best biblical loop-the-loops. You want to dazzle, razzle and impress the crowds. But, friend, you are not a stunt pilot. And there are no crowds – only passengers who have paid their money and are expecting you to get them from A to B safely and happily. Also, as I've said before, whilst it's true that the take-off and landing may be the most dangerous parts of a flight, any good pilot knows that the real work is done in level flight.

I used to own a flight simulator; not one of those super-duper ones that are on hydraulic stilts, but rather one on my PC. It was pretty neat. Controlling the plane was important, but so was listening to air traffic announcements and making smooth controlled turns. You've probably got me down as some sort of sad man by now so can I say – in my defence – I *used* to own one.

Other than poking fun at myself, the point of the story is this: level flight for me as a desk-pilot was incredibly *boring*. Nothing much seemed to happen; I could go away and make a cup of coffee and still come back to an unchanged screen. In fact, there was even a button which accelerated time to get this boring part out of the way and speed to the more interesting landing phase.

I've no doubt that some of my own listeners have sometimes wished there were such a button in my own preaching! Nevertheless, it is in level flight that the distance is covered. My London Heathrow to Washington Dulles flight took me eight hours. Twenty minutes of that were take-off and ascent. The final thirty minutes were descent and landing. That means that almost 90% of the eight-hour flight was spent steadily and deliberately making our way towards the destination.

It's in level flight that your talk work is going to be done. Sure, the take-off-introduction will be a great moment as you get folks into the air. And (as we shall see) the landing needs to be safe and solid. But it's this middle part that really, really counts.

Let me put it another way. You can start badly, and even finish badly, but still deliver a good talk overall. However, if the middle section's content is not there, even the best introduction and sparkiest ending will leave your hearers cold and empty. They may not feel cold and empty, but if you have not given them the substance of the Bible, then you have given them nothing of value. Your task, as pilot of this Bible talk, is to get the truth from the page of the Bible to the heart of your hearers. Get that bit wrong and your Bible talk is not a Bible talk at all.

DEPEND ON THE COMPANY

Now how do you make that transition – from the Bible page to the person? How, in other words, do you get to people's hearts?

You do it through open minds. In other words, the truth of God's word needs to be understood in order to be really felt. The two are very closely connected: you can't really *feel* the impact of something in the Bible unless you've *understood* it. However, when it comes to spiritual truth and the Christian, neither can you simply *understand* something without it having a profound effect on how you *feel*.

Your level-flight work therefore needs to take Bible truths and both explain and apply them to people's hearts through their spiritually enlightened minds. That sounds a tall order, doesn't it? But here's one of the great and encouraging truths of Bible ministry: what I've just described is not really your job at all but God's.

A pilot is the paid employee of the company, so the company is going to use them. But, at the end of the flight, they want people to say how great the company was and what a great job the company did! My flight to Washington – unusually – was with Virgin Atlantic. I don't fly much, but when I do, I tend to fly BA. However, for this trip I could only get a cheap flight with the young upstarts. Yet I was really quite pleasantly surprised. The food was good (and I need a strange diet). The plane was new. The staff were helpful. It was all good, in fact. So when I got home, I raved about the company because it was the company that pleased me. But I said nothing about the pilot and I've completely forgotten his name – Captain Jones or something similar, I imagine.

And those of us who are piloting the Bible talks are doing so in complete and utter dependence on The Company: in our case, the Holy Trinity of Father, Son and Spirit. It is God himself whom we count on to be at work. Yes, for a brief moment, we're flying the plane and operating the controls. But in reality, we are Company men and women and the humanly impossible task of making things stick in hearer's minds and hearts is not our own but the Spirit's.

That doesn't mean we sit back and do nothing. My pilot worked hard for us. That's exactly the hard-working language we've seen in 2 Timothy. Rather, it means that we are not to be overwhelmed with the task of getting from the page to the heart of hearers. Without wanting to be too reductionistic, let me put it like this: we do our job; the Spirit does his. That's why prayer is such an important element of preparation.

As I've already said, this book is not about the processes that are helpful to go through when trying to understand and proclaim a passage. At the end I suggest some other books which can help you with that. Rather, this book is about giving the talk itself. So I want to concentrate on some practical helps which I believe and hope will make your talk better, and will make the most of the hard work I am sure you have already done in getting to grips with a passage.

HAVE A FLIGHT PLAN

It never ceases to amaze me how smooth flying is, even though my last two flights took me over thousands and thousands of miles. I love keeping up to date with the little screen map in front of my seat that shows you where you are and where you've come from. I love seeing famous place names slip by. In fact, for those on the ground, there's even a website (flightradar24.com) where you can track flights over your head and see where they've come from and where they're going. Either map, though, shows the same extraordinary thing: how remarkably few turns a modern plane takes. When an aircraft sets out from London to, say, Delhi, it may change direction only once or twice.

Another key to a smooth, gentle, happy flight is smooth, gentle, happy changes. No one wants abrupt turns or steep banks, or announcements saying, 'Fasten your seat belts, ladies and gentlemen, we're about to make a turn.' Rather, passengers are hoping for changes which are so discreet that it's only when you notice that the position of the sun has changed that you realise you've altered direction at all.

A good Bible talk needs a smooth flight plan. It needs a structure that will get hearers from A to B in a straightforward manner. The structure should reflect the passage (in other words, it's the passage that should be driving things along).

It will sometimes need to change direction, but the changes should be so smooth and gentle that if people don't notice them, that's fine.

I've never flown an actual plane, but I've got a rough idea how it works. When a plane is in flight, direction changes are often made through the autopilot. The captain can dial in a new compass direction and the plane management systems automatically tip the wings to bring the aircraft on to its new heading. Of course, an experienced pilot can do that himself just as well. But I guess a novice would be tempted to be like a first-timer driving a car: they'd be much too likely to use sharp movements on the stick rather than the gentle banking that is needed to turn a jumbo smoothly.

Do you see the point? I can easily listen to a three-point sermon. But it is going to feel like three sermons superglued together unless the changes from one point to another are seamless and gentle. I never forget one of my mentors telling me early on in my preaching to give time in preparation to how points transition from one to another: it was one of the most helpful preaching lessons I ever learnt. A sermon which contains the line, 'That was my first point. Now, my next point is ...' where there is no connection between the ideas is neither gentle nor helpful for listeners.

Don't get me wrong. You may still get the listeners to the destination. But it will not be a smooth journey and so – unless you really have no choice – why fly the plane that way? To put it another way, for some long-haul destinations it's often much cheaper to fly via Dubai or Dohar. But no regular traveller wants to choose that option over non-stop travel unless they really have to. So a disjointed talk can still work, but why fly such abrupt legs when you could be going non-stop?

When you're preparing, therefore, think of how the talk fits together. Try to put yourself in the shoes of a hearer. Does one point flow into another? Is there a connection which will help people to feel they are on one journey? How will I actually end one point and introduce the next?

Let me give you an example. I recently preached through Luke 5:27–39. At first glance it looks like two stories: first the story of Jesus eating with Levi (vv. 27–32), then Jesus answering a question about fasting (vv. 33–39). However, on closer inspection the stories are intimately linked. The first story is about a feast leading to repentance. That's the theme with which the story ends. Jesus is then immediately questioned about fasting. Why? Because repentance in the Old Testament is often linked with sorrowful fasting, and yet here are the disciples of Jesus whooping it up, which doesn't seem right. What kind of repentance is that?

The answer is that it is the kind of repentance which doesn't require fasting because it's ultimately joyful: the bridegroom (that is, Jesus) is with the people and there's no cause for sorrow. It's a great little passage. I'm not going to preach it to you now. However, I hope you can see there is a transition between the two sections in the text itself (in this case *repentance*), and it is finding and using that link that gave (I hope) my two-point sermon a smooth transition from point one (which covered vv. 27–32) to point two (v. 33 onwards).

GIVE PEOPLE A SMOOTH FLIGHT

It's not just gentle turns that make a flight smooth. Changes in height and variations in speed should be gradual to avoid causing disruption. I was once travelling on a plane which dropped a thousand feet very abruptly. It was, I understood later, because of some kind of air pocket, which is not uncommon and for which planes are built and pilots are trained. But it scared the daylights out of me. It was totally unexpected and left my stomach churning and my heart rapidly beating. The point is this: smooth flying is achieved not only by gentle turns. The best flights are smooth in every sense: nothing abrupt or stomach-churning.

Now you can hopefully see that, pushed too far, this could make for some pretty boring sermons! I'm not arguing a case for monotones and dreary delivery!

No one enjoys listening to sermons like that, they don't keep the attention of the audience and therefore much of what the speaker has to convey is lost on them. In contrast, changes in tone and volume can be used very effectively to add emphasis, drama and emotion, thus fully engaging the listener and enhancing the key truths.

Nevertheless, to be able to listen to someone preaching or teaching, there does need to be a consistency about their delivery. For example, changes in tone and volume can be used very effectively in a sermon. Too many changes in tone and volume, and too sharp a distinction, can simply diminish the message. If hearers have to strain to hear you in the quiet passages, then it's not going to do a lot of good. Similarly, if you suddenly shout at the top of your voice unexpectedly, all you're going to do is to give the PA operators a mild heart attack.

So add variation? Yes! But go to extremes? No! This applies to volume and pace.

Very often inexperienced speakers speak more quickly in the parts of their talk where they are most comfortable. That's often because they don't feel so bound by notes. Then they slow up in the parts they are less sure of, often resorting to reading from their script itself. If you've ever listened to a sermon or talk like that, you will know that it is a hard thing to listen to. You've just got yourself attuned to one pace and suddenly the speaker is off on another one.

Ironically, it is often the parts of the talk that speakers are most familiar with (and therefore deliver most quickly), which are also the best parts. So the less important sections get delivered slowly and deliberately whilst the real big hitters get gabbled out with no chance for hearers to digest what is being said. As I say, that's ironic, because if you would expect to make an error in this area, it would probably be the other way around.

Let me say one other thing about height changes. Level flight is best done when it is ... level. Let's push the picture a bit. Assume your flight level (height above ground) is a measure of the kind of academic level you've built into your talk. By academic level I mean the kind of understanding you've assumed of your listeners. Maybe you've assumed they're all keen Christians who know their Bibles well. That may well be true, and at one level it makes your Bible talk a whole lot easier. But maybe you've got brand-new baby Christians. Maybe they can't follow cross references because they simply don't know their Bibles.

A Bible talk is easiest, let's be honest, if your listeners are all in the same boat. But in most normal churches and settings that's unlikely to be the case.

You're more likely to be speaking to a mixed lot. There's a great temptation therefore to go from the complex to the simple and back again. Back and forth you go, for example with, 'If you're interested, this word in Greek means ....' for the clever dudes, followed the next minute by, 'Turn to Genesis, that's the very first book of the Bible' for the newbies.

For the record, those giving Bible talks often confuse achieving simplicity with exploring how deep something is. Investigating something in depth is not about quoting Greek and Hebrew, or highlighting passage bookends (if you even know what those are). Going deep is to do with discovering God himself: his character, nature and work. And your task is to be deep yet simple.

My rule of thumb is to assume that every congregation has some baby Christians in it, or even those who are not yet Christians. It's good to help them through your talk. And even those who are mature could use a little help. Don't, however, think that means you can't go for depth.

Oh, and – unless it's really unavoidable – stay away from impressing people with Greek. What pilot have you ever heard come on the intercom and tell you, 'Don't worry folks, you'll be glad to know that the pitot tubes are working just fine and we've got a static port and angle of attack vane just helping us along there'? (I'm making most of this stuff up.)

The passengers don't need to know this information. They need this matter to be working in the background, but they don't need to know about it. Ninety-nine times out of a hundred it's the same for languages. You may be using commentaries which refer liberally to Hebrew, Aramaic and Greek. You may even know what they're talking about. If so, use the information in your preparation. But don't feel – especially as a novice captain – that you need to give your listeners the same diet.

AVOID TURBULENCE!

Have you ever asked a long-distance traveller about a flight they've just been on? Very often they say, 'It was pretty smooth', but sometimes they comment, 'It was a bit bumpy.' In fact, if anyone has flown and experienced turbulence, they nearly *always* remember it. It sticks in the brain and, after a while, begins to define the flight itself.

So the best pilots, when they can, avoid turbulence. My pilot friends tell me that they do this with careful advance planning. They look out for weather patterns and listen to the stories of others who have flown the same route recently. Then in their preparation they plan the flight to try to avoid the worst disruptions.

Friend, your talk needs to do the same. Avoid adding in turbulence – that is controversy which need not be there in the first place. No Bible speaker should be doing that, but plenty do, often because they have their own pet subjects – hates or loves – which they love to get across. It's amazing how they can twist individual scriptures and just end up saying the same thing over and over.

But let's assume you're a pilot with a bit more integrity than that. You're not going to go out actively looking for trouble. However, your passage may contain some tricky ideas and issues that may cause some stirring. What do you do with these? The answer is that you go with the flow of the passage: your job is to get people from A to B, just as the passage gets them from A to B. You have no right to choose a different destination, or even a different route. Nevertheless, you want to do it in such a way that causes the least turbulence.

Let me take you back to my recent sermon on Luke 5:27–39. If you glanced at the passage before, you'll see that Jesus makes some strong statements about fasting. He backs his teaching up with lessons about the New Covenant being different from the Old (vv. 33–39). Now, this teaching could be turbulent for some of your listeners.

They may, for example, come from a culture where fasting is more than prevalent – in some cultures it has become a rather legalistic and meaningless part of the Christian life. What do you say to such people? Perhaps, 'You've completely got it wrong, you sinners!'? Well, that would certainly be direct! You've recognised the challenge of the passage to a certain extent (which is that the coming of Jesus changes Old Testament practice in some way), but – I would suggest – you've blown it. You've not anticipated the turbulence your remarks have caused, nor have you done anything to help people digest the lesson you think the passage is making. So when those folk get home, what's their lasting impression? 'It was a pretty bumpy ride,' they say, and they remember nothing about repentance, the bridegroom or the nature of the New Covenant; all they remember is the way you beat them up about fasting.

For what it is worth, it is always easier when speaking to beat people up rather than build them up. The former needs less skill than the latter. I think the Bible does both, but – as we saw in 2 Timothy – even the correction is couched in terms of language that is positive: 'rebuking, correcting and training in righteousness' (3:16). A good Bible speaker learns to do those things in a way which is, well, Christian.

PREPARE EARLY FOR LANDING

There's one more thing to say about level flight. It's this: the captain of the plane is always getting you ready for the final destination. It may be so subtle you don't notice it, but, for example, if you listen carefully you'll find that midway through the flight he will tell you the temperature and weather at the destination. He'll tell you how long it will be until landing and therefore how long you've got to freshen up and so on. He'll give you a time check at your point of arrival so you can set your watch properly. All the time, in sometimes small but significant, ways, the pilot is getting you ready to be on the ground.

That is also how a Bible talk needs to work. All the time you're getting people ready for the end. All the time you should be thinking through how the whole thing is going to come to a climax. For Bible talks that means with application. Remember, your role as speaker is to get from the page of the text to the heart of the hearers.

Ultimately, that implies not just asking, 'What does this *mean*?' but 'What *difference* does this make?' We call that application and it is a very important part of Bible talks. Helping people understand a passage is only part of the work. If we are filling people's heads with knowledge but missing their hearts, then something is wrong. Of course, understanding is an important step – but it's a step that someone giving a talk needs to go beyond.

Sometimes that application will be very simple. For an appropriate passage in an evangelistic meeting, it might be asking people to believe in the gospel. For other passages in other settings, it will be more complex. There may be something to do, for example.

However, whatever your circumstances, I'm a great believer in working towards that application as soon as is practically appropriate. It might seem easier for you to prepare a talk which gives fifteen minutes to explanation and then five minutes to application, but much of the time that's going to sound a little stilted to listeners, and so they're not really going to be drawn in. Furthermore, most Bible passages don't work that way. Rather, they imply applications as they go.

Take my Luke 5 passage again. Even in the first half there are issues of leaving everything and following Jesus (vv. 27–28); issues to do with eating and drinking with sinners and sharing the good news (vv. 29–30); and issues to do with the mission of Jesus (vv. 31–32). These applications have most force when they are tied to the verses from which they are derived.

Let me extend the plane analogy a little. Suppose the captain says something like, 'If you look out of the window, you will be able to see the beautiful sunrise. You might like to know it's also sunny at our destination.' There is an immediate connection between the present reality (the sunrise seen out of the window) and the weather at the port of arrival (sunshine). The application is not abstract from the original information and therefore carries greater weight.

If I had waited until the end of the sermon to apply the Bible, I could have given people five main points of application. Even if my listeners could have remembered them all, they would been divorced from the text by such a distance that they would have lost their force. At worst, they would have seemed like things Adrian had dreamt up.

So level flight is key; it's the heart of your talk. It deserves most of your preparation and attention. And it is where your talk stands or falls. Perhaps the beginning and ending will be punchier and more glamorous. But it's in level flight where the real work is done, as every captain knows.

He also knows, however, that you've still got to land the plane. And that's where we go to next ...

LANDING

'TAKE YOUR SEATS FOR LANDING'

We're almost home. There's a sense of relief on a plane when the trays are cleared away, the seats are returned to the upright position and the 'Fasten your seat belts' sign is illuminated. It's not long now until the plane will be on the ground and we will have reached our destination. Here's the thing, however: we're not home yet. We've not arrived until the plane is safely on the ground and has taxied to the gate. Likewise a Bible talk is not over until listeners are left thinking about what the main teaching and application is for them personally.

There are certain procedures that are worth following in a good landing – though of course, you don't want every conclusion to every sermon to be the same. The most important is to reinforce the key takeaway points. What is it that you are hoping people will remember and do as a result of this talk? You should have already told them, but it's worth repeating it just to make sure that people remember what you've planned that they will remember. If you have had some turbulence, perhaps unexpected, here's the place to put things right.

My personal preference is to try to link in with the introduction if at all possible. This isn't, strictly speaking, absolutely necessary, but it gives a sense of journeying and learning together if folk can be reminded where they started. Remember my Luke 5 sermon? As it's all about Jesus' new way, my introduction was framed around asking people what they thought of new things. I ended in the same way: 'So here is something new which blows everything else away.' That's all it needed – some point of connection with where we started off.

However, don't feel that you have to go over everything again in the landing phase. Remember that most of the work done and distance covered comes in level flight. You do not have time (and your listeners almost certainly do not have the energy) to do it all again.

Nor is there a need to give people new information. When the descent begins, people want to get ready for landing. They don't want new destinations or changes in direction. It's the same with a Bible talk. It's perfectly possible, of course, to introduce new ideas into a conclusion, but I believe it rarely works or adds to the hard work already done. So at this stage, avoid anything revolutionary.

LAND QUICKLY!

That brings us neatly to our next top tip for a Bible talk pilot: try to land the plane quickly. In fact, long descents and endless circling around just make passengers more nervous. At busy times, planes sometimes join what are called stacks where planes essentially queue for a landing slot. Being on a plane at times like that can be immensely frustrating. I have been in a stack near London where I have been able to see London through the window as we have circled around; in some ways it would have been better to have been in the clouds and unaware of my position. There's nothing more frustrating than being almost home, but never quite landing.

So don't let your hearers get drawn into endless circling. I heard a sermon the other day which had a really good beginning and a strong central section. However, the end of the sermon just went on and on and on. I'm sure it wasn't just me at the end thinking, 'Just land the plane, will you?'

Endings that are too long generally reflect speakers who are not really confident in what they wanted to say in the main part of the talk. They feel they have to keep adding and adding to improve things. So if your talk conclusion looks long, it probably means you need to go back to the drawing board for level flight.

BUT NOT TOO QUICKLY!

There's a flip side to this piece of advice though. A good, steady, speedy descent is critical. But don't try to come in too fast.

Here's a good piece of aeroplane trivia for you: the average descent into an airport in the UK is, I'm told, at a 3° angle. That does not feel really very much at all when you're on the plane. No one sits hanging on to their straps with the plane in a nosedive. You can still walk the aisles (if you're allowed). Yet you still get to the ground pretty quickly – it took just twenty minutes to come down into Heathrow on my flight.

The key is to come down quickly but not too quickly. If you want to bring your hearers safely home, then first make sure there's not too much circling around. Second, ensure that your descent is controlled and gentle.

I've heard sermons (you probably have too) which end so abruptly it's like being woken from a deep sleep. Fair enough, in some of them I may actually have been asleep. But abruptness – for the most part – doesn't help the speaker's cause. It's a bit like turbulence – it becomes the only thing that people remember.

Endings that are too short generally reflect speakers who have put too much talking time into level flight.

They've used up every single second of their allotted time (and then some). Someone at the back is probably making a chopping sign across the neck to speed them up. So, bump! The plane lands with an abruptness that catches people's breath.

TAKE THEM TO THE GATE

Your job is not quite completed yet. You may have landed the plane, but there is still some taxiing to be done. All the hard work may be over, but the work is not actually finished until the plane is safely at the gate and the passengers are disembarking. A good Bible speaker takes people all the way to their destination point. He joins the dots for people, helping them, for example, begin to work out applications in their own lives. In the same way no pilot leaves his passengers stranded on the runway but takes them right up to the air bridge and waits for the doors to be opened.

In fact, why not take a leaf out of the old training book for pilots. I know that aircraft captains don't do this anymore, but in the more glamorous days of flight, the captain would be there at the door saying goodbye and making himself available to people who wanted to chat. There's a lot to be said for that.

Of course I don't mean standing at the door like some automaton. In the *Toy Story 2* film, Air-Hostess-Barbie just has one phrase and it's pretty comical: 'Bye-bye now. Bye-bye now. Bye-bye now.' Please don't utter that kind of goodbye.

Instead, give your people the kind of old-fashioned, first-class service where the captain takes his turn to make sure the passengers are happy: their questions are answered and their objections are overturned. Some people do that at the door, others mingle; do whatever suits your situation and character best. Make sure you find time to do it, however, for you may have noticed that this hard work you've just put yourself through is actually not for you; it's for them. Remember: 'To fly. To serve.'

ARRIVALS

Congratulations, you've arrived.

I once was a passenger on a flight piloted by Tony Underwood. For those of you under forty (probably most of you), Tony was an England rugby international in the days when the game was amateur. I believe he started off as an RAF pilot and then switched on rugby retirement into commercial flying.

As far as I can remember, the flight was no less or more eventful for having a famous captain. In fact, my only worry was that this captain was going to be so self-confident he might cut some dangerous corners or be tempted to impress us with some hands-off flying. I'm happy to report that my fear was entirely unfounded.

I've since flown on that same airline several times and I've never had Tony fly me again. But I've arrived safely at my destination every time. That's the thing with flying. You don't need to be with a famous captain to enjoy the ride.

This is my encouragement for you. You're not John Piper, nor Tim Keller, nor Vaughan Roberts, nor – thank God – Adrian Reynolds. In all probability, you are not as famous as at least some of these people. You may not even be as able – not everyone is equally gifted by God to do this task. Yet you still have an important role: it's to speak the Bible faithfully and (I hope) engagingly, thus carefully taking your hearers to the destination that God intends.

Once God spoke through a donkey. There's certainly hope for you and I. With careful and prayerful preparation, and with the help of the Holy Spirit, the talk you are about to give may have exactly the same effect, or even better, than if Piper, Keller or Roberts was standing in front of your audience.

You are the one who has been called to serve these people right now. You are the pilot. May you know the Spirit's help and confidence. And may you speak God's word faithfully. May, in other words, your people arrive at the right destination.

FURTHER READING

Here are four simple books which I believe you will find of enormous help in tackling the 'how to' element of giving a talk.

1. **Expositional Preaching** by David Helm (Crossway, 2014). This is one of my favourite books on preaching, which is hardly surprising as it is based largely on instructions and lessons from The Proclamation Trust where I work. Dave has a great way of explaining things simply with basic diagrams that illuminate rather than confuse. It's only a short book (115 small pages) but contains some real gems to get you started.
2. **Preaching Pure and Simple** by Stuart Olyott (Bryntirion Press, 2005). Stuart is a very experienced preacher and his introductory book on preaching covers all the bases. It's practical and – this is what I really like – does not ignore the spiritual nature of preaching.
3. **Preaching?: Simple Teaching on Simply Preaching** by Alec Motyer (Christian Focus, 2013). Alec is another experienced preacher who has produced this very useful little volume about simple preaching. I've found it enormously helpful and I know you will too.

4. **Gospel Centred Preaching** by Tim Chester and Marcus Honeysett (The Good Book Company, 2014). Tim and Marcus' book is perhaps the most practical of these four – it is almost a kind of workbook with questions to reflect on and apply to a passage. Like the others, it's simple and effective and is highly recommended.

MORE IN THIS SERIES

ON BEING A SERVANT OF GOD
Warren Wiersbe
978-1-910587-10-2

THE CALL
Paul Mallard & Trevor Archer
978-1-910587-50-8

WHY FREE CHURCH MINISTRY?
Graham Beynon
978-1-910587-49-2